MW00721320

ALSO BY SHARON POLLOCK

Blood Relations
(in *Modern Canadian Plays*, vol. 1)

Walsh

ON SHARON POLLOCK'S LIFE AND WORK

Making Theatre: A Life of Sharon Pollock
by Sherrill Grace

All published by Talonbooks

Saucy Jack

A Play

Sharon Pollock

Talonbooks

Talonbooks
9259 Shaughnessy Street, Vancouver, British Columbia, Canada V6P 6R4
talonbooks.com

Talonbooks is located on xʷməθkʷəy̓əm, Sḵwx̱wú7mesh, and səl̓ilwətaʔɬ Lands

First printing: 2022

Typeset in Minion
Printed and bound in Canada on 100% post-consumer recycled paper

Cover and interior design by Typesmith

Talonbooks acknowledges the financial support of the Canada Council for the Arts, the Government of Canada through the Canada Book Fund, and the Province of British Columbia through the British Columbia Arts Council and the Book Publishing Tax Credit.

LIBRARY AND ARCHIVES CANADA CATALOGUING IN PUBLICATION

Title: Saucy Jack : a play / Sharon Pollock.
Names: Pollock, Sharon, author.
Description: Previously published: Winnipeg: Blizzard Publishing, 1994.
Identifiers: Canadiana 20220430977 | ISBN 9781772015287 (softcover)
Classification: LCC PS8581.O34 S38 2022 | DDC C812/.54—dc23

Playwright's Note

I'm uncertain what drew me to Jack the Ripper as raw material, but then I am never able to map the process whereby casual interest in an event or individuals is transformed into fanatical absorption, and eventually, a play. I realize that I don't so much choose the play I write as it chooses me, and Jack, for whatever reason, has had me by the neck for a long time. I do know I was not, and am not, interested in putting forth a personal theory as to his identity. This play is more an extrapolation and variation mixing historical characters, probable relationships, and possible events with "What if?" in an effort to explore a human equation of now.

And I'm not particularly interested in the why of the original Ripper murders. I suppose that's either because it is ultimately unknowable, or because I find it to be thus: the women are killed because they can be killed with relative or complete impunity. It's done because it can be done. That reason is sufficient for those who undertake such actions. The end or objective or motivation for the re-enactment of the women's deaths in the play is not to achieve the death of the women, but to achieve some other end or objective that relates to the relationship between the men. "Love," "loyalty," "friendship" are words the men use, but the actions through which such noble sentiments manifest themselves are the ones of betrayal, duplicity, and murder. When Kate tries to warn and inform Montague of the danger through subtle language, even in code you might say, from which he could deduce the true situation, he chooses to ally himself with Eddy, believing his knowledge of Jem's, and possibly Eddy's, guilt will enable him to further his own interests. And in so doing, he drinks up and dies. Kate proves an avenue of survival for Montague, which he rejects. I see her then as "Able to Leave," but not before providing a glimpse of the future, and the ultimate failure and demise of the supposedly "Dominant," be they of class or sex. I am less interested in whether Jem or Eddy, or some combination of them, and possibly others, are indeed guilty of the murders than I am interested in the whys and ways Jem attempts to bind Eddy to him, as well as to confirm or negate his fearful suspicions regarding his own role in the Ripper events. He's caught in a terrible dilemma. If he is indeed guilty of the crimes, he is "sane," for his clouded recall is founded on reality. If he is innocent of the crimes, his memory and mind are serving up false data, and he's "insane." The production must know who's guilty, but Jem does not. The only murder for which guilt can be assigned with certainty is Montague's.

I'm interested in Kate's ability, as she acquires knowledge by listening and observing, to play the role of the various victims assigned to her but, within this playing of the role, to use it against those who've assigned the role. In the first act, she speaks when commanded to speak or has permission to speak. Gradually, she initiates speech. When she is silent in the second act, it is she who chooses silence, and that silence comes with knowledge. She will choose when she speaks, and why.

The extrapolation and variation provide the means to trace the woman's evolution from a silent, unknown, nameless figure (although I name her in the cast list) to the only vital or potent figure or force in the play when the final blackout occurs. Her exploitation has not victimized her; it has empowered her. She is larger than herself at the end. The men, while attempting to shift, gain, trade, and manipulate power between themselves (sometimes using her as the means to do so) are rendered impotent by their actions and become smaller than themselves. She lives. They die.

SHARON POLLOCK
September 1994

Production History

Saucy Jack was first produced by the Garry Theatre, Calgary, Alberta, on November 25, 1993, with the following cast:

JEM	Jarvis Hall
KATE	Rae Ellen Bodie
EDDY	Brian Johnston
MONTAGUE	Brent Weaver

Director: Sharon Pollock

Assistant Director and Fight Director: Paul Gelineau

Set designer: K.C. Campbell

Lighting designer: Craig Hansen

Costume and prop designer: Christopher Foreman

Stage Manager: Tim Culbert

Assistant Stage Manager: Andrew Ross

Characters

JEM: James Kenneth Stephen, the former Cambridge tutor and intimate friend of Prince Albert Victor; twenty-nine years old.

EDDY: Prince Albert Victor, grandson of Queen Victoria and heir to the throne of England; mid twenties.

KATE: A music hall entertainer and actor; thirty-five years old.

MONTAGUE: Montague Druitt, a tutor and teacher at a prestigious boy's school; late twenties.

Act 1

Chiswick, England.

Saturday, December 1, 1888. About 8:00 p.m.

A room in a house on the Thames. The house is the weekend getaway of Henry Wilson, a senior bureaucrat at the Home Office, a government department equivalent to our Department of Justice.

Upstage centre is a pair of French doors that open onto a veranda that runs across the back of the house. The doors are locked. From the veranda, the grounds run down to the river. On the inside, the doors open onto an interior level with two steps down into the room.

There is a fireplace on one wall. A sideboard holds glasses and decanters of liquor amongst other things.

There are various pieces of furniture in the room: chairs, a large circular pouffe, a small table, etc. This includes two chairs, one extreme stage right, the other extreme stage left; they face each other. There are several large plants in the room. All but the fireplace, sideboard, and plants, are covered by crimson dust sheets.

There is a faint light in the room and the crimson sheets seem to glow. A figure, JEM, enters up the veranda steps, unlocks the French doors, looks into the room without entering, steps back as if checking the exterior look of the place, enters somewhat tentatively, and closes the French doors, unintentionally leaving them a bit ajar. He carries a parcel wrapped in newsprint about eighteen by eight inches in size.

His gaze moves over the crimson dust sheets and rests on the sheet nearest him. He looks under the dust sheet, discovers a chair, lifts the sheet off the chair, and drops it on the floor.

The light on some of the dust sheets grows somewhat hotter. JEM slowly approaches them, studies them for a moment, then removes his overcoat and puts it on the chair from which he has removed the dust sheet. He slowly looks around the room, then turns to take in the items on the top of the sideboard. He returns to study the two hotter dust sheets. One is fairly large – the one covering the pouffe. He stares at it, then turns to the second which covers a chair and a small table. He lifts a corner of the sheet and sees a chair leg. He sits in the chair without removing the dust sheet. He sits still for a moment holding the parcel protectively. After a moment he becomes aware of the parcel, looks to the extension of the dust sheet beside him, feels it, and lifts a corner of it to reveal the small table. He places the parcel under the sheet on top of the small table and sits back in the chair. He removes his hat, casually and slowly he rubs his head just above the hair line around the right temple. He replaces his hat on his head.

He thinks a moment, looks back on the French doors, checks a pocket watch, thinks for a moment, looks towards the French doors, snaps the watch closed and returns it to his pocket. He sits for a bit thinking. He pulls a handkerchief from his pocket which turns out to be red, very close if not identical to the colour of the dust sheets. He looks from the handkerchief to the dust sheets, puts the handkerchief away, feels his pockets looking for perhaps the right handkerchief. He can't find it. He sits for a moment, looks back to the French doors. He sits for a while. He speaks.

JEM

First ... first, and last ... I have a plan.
Execute, the plan ... first and last ...
De ... Kember
De Kember?

December! Decemberdecember, I don't like December, I don't like
winter, I don't ... like ...

Saturday! I like Saturday, I like weekends, I like Friday and
Saturday and Sunday, I don't like December, I like weekends,
I like ...

There's always a lot to *dooo* on a weekend, there's always ... there's
always ... Friends! I have a lot of friends and I see them on the
weekends, I see my friends on the weekends, on the weekends I
see them –

> *KATE has come up the steps. She pushes open one of the
> French doors and enters the room. She carries a carpet
> bag. JEM is unaware of her presence.*

on Friday and Saturday and Sunday, I –

> *KATE puts her carpet bag down, JEM pauses.*

I ... hear things, I hear things I –

> *JEM turns, he sees KATE who smiles. He turns back
> ignoring her.*

I see things I ...

I do things, yes I do, I do, I do things I –

> *He laughs, glancing towards the parcel concealed by the
> dust sheet on the table. He stops himself from laughing.*

Excuse me.

> *He looks back at KATE, then goes to her.*

It's because I don't like December, it reminds me of winter, it *is*
winter for Christ's sake, December is winter!

However –

3

I can be charming, many people have told me I'm charming, I am charming, that can be a terrible burden you know, how the hell would you know – you aren't charming, I am charming you are not charming, you are not even here for Christ's sake!

He returns to his chair.

I am here.
I am here the year –
Please –

He beckons for KATE to join him, she does and sits on the pouffe still covered by the dust sheet.

The year is, don't tell me, I know. I know what the year is, this particular year, this year is, 1888, Saturday December December the …

KATE holds up one finger.

First! Yes December the first Saturday 1888 and I'll tell you why I hate winter and why I hate weekends – you thought you knew how I felt about weekends but what I said before wasn't true, well, partially true – but why I hate winter, look …

He removes his hat, carefully places it on the dust-sheeted table, pushes back his hair, and tilts his head forward as if to display some area of injury on his head to KATE.

It doesn't hurt.
No, it doesn't hurt.

It has left me unimpaired, I was fortunate in a way, it happened, in winter, in winter but not in December, dismember dis –
Remember *not* … in … winter. I was riding, a horse, of course and I came on a wind sail and I stopped the horse to this side of the wind sail which was turning, like they do … they … and the horse backed … up … into the path of the … turning blade … blade …

His gaze rests on the table on which the parcel lies concealed by the dust sheet. Pause.

What was I saying?

KATE makes a turning gesture with her hand.

And I hit my head! It hit my head and my head was injured and the stupid bloody horse got away scot-free!

He laughs; notices KATE isn't laughing.

The horse was not injured.

KATE indicates with a small nod that she understands this.

Or else ... There was an erection a – an erection, a turning ... blade ... over a wall, a pumping mill worked by a small wind-wheel which I wished which I ... *wished* ... to examine and in so doing either by accident or ... design received a blow to the head which you may observe and the horse was, or was not, present in this re-counting of the event. Which ... is why I hate winter! This happened in winter, I said that, although not in December ... To the best of my knowledge ...

which
is a bit spotty
around this particular event
although ...

He gives KATE a roll of money.

It is unimpaired otherwise, you may judge for yourself.

He moves to the sideboard and rearranges some items on it.

Although some individuals do take note of the site of the injury whether it be on the horse or the head or that erection I was telling you about, I really don't know, I don't remember, I have to rely on what I read or what others tell me and I really don't care and it really doesn't matter!!

JEM looks at KATE, who is intent on counting the money. He looks at the French doors, goes over and locks them. He looks at KATE who is putting the money away, and puts the key on the sideboard. KATE, finished with her money business, looks at JEM. He speaks.

I come from a long line of brilliant people, on my mother's side of a higher moral and religious character than on the paternal, where intellectual activity and achievement are held in the highest esteem, and my father, Judge Fitzjames Stephen, is revered and admired and admired and revered and will go a bit bonky at the end of his life I'm fairly certain of that!!

Pause.

And my cousin is Virginia Woolf, what more can I say? You no doubt are in a position to know more of her than I do and I no doubt will die in a booby hatch diagnosed as suffering from a manic-depressive illness, believing a warrant out for my detention – my having committed some... unspecified... crime... -es, crimes – and refusing all food since hearing of my dear friend Prince Eddy's death from... influenza or neurosyphilis or... something like that on... January 14, 1892, my own death occurring on... February the third... twenty days after Eddy's. You see it's all winter, everything's winter, there's something behind that but I don't want to go into it now!

Now...

Pause.

Do those days fall on a weekend, that is the question!

Pause.

I don't know.

Pause.

The question.
I know the question I don't know the answer! The answer?
I don't know.

How the hell would I know? I'm just waiting for Eddy, Prince... Albert... Victor!

He suddenly gets up and takes in the room and comes to a realization.

This is Harry F. Wilson's house! It's Harry's house, I'm quite certain of that, yes and he's...

Important! You know, all of my friends – and I have quite a lot of them – are important you know, and he, Harry that is, is an Undersecretary at the Home Office to someone whose name I won't mention but who's rather important and a friend of my father's and, of course, between Harry and my father and my father and Harry and all of my important friends I hear quite a bit!

Pause.

About things!... That interest me!... That are to my benefit!... And Eddy's benefit!... And Montague Druitt's benefit, whom you haven't heard of yet although I don't care much about Montague's benefit, I don't give a shit about him I don't care for him, I care superficially for him he is not a friend a friend he's not!

He belongs to...
Is a member of...
December remember dismember –
Well life is life is, he's a member of...
a group of
friends who
come together
come at any rate
God!!!

> *He heaves a great sigh, sinks into the chair, and after a moment makes a small gesture towards his head. Pause.*

I would blow up the Houses of Parliament and slit the throats of all my so-called friends if it bought a moment's peace!

> *KATE unobtrusively gets up and very casually and slowly begins to make her way towards the French doors.*

But of course I can't... Yes I can... do that, do it!

> *JEM notices KATE has moved and moves to join her.*

Besides I like them, they are dear to me but I can see the necessity, the theoretical necessity if things are to change, what things? I don't know, I had it there for a minute but it's gone now...

Ah well...

One does what one can, one does... what one has to... to help things along, to gain a moment's pleasure, God knows that's difficult enough, you have to keep your wits about you. You mustn't believe anything I say, I don't believe a thing I say, I just listen, I keep my mouth shut and I listen and I can't believe what

I'm hearing I can't believe it! but I do it, I do it anyway, I do it for Eddy! He is a very special person and must be protected, sacrifices must be made. You can understand that. History will understand that, except all this morbid talk of his dying and my dying is depressing, particularly for a manic depressive which I don't believe I am, but the thought of Montague popping off is quite a jolly thought which I must try and suppress.

Pause. He looks at KATE.

A mask is more interesting than the face. Someone said that. Or they will. I understand we must die, Eddy and I, but not quite yet, others first... others... first... first – of December! Now I remember! I hate it when that happens! Chiswick!

Harry's place is in Chiswick! This place is in Chiswick. Although Harry isn't here, he's too smart for that! Saturday December the first 1888 everything happens on weekends!

In winter!

Not always in winter. The first was in August, the first was on the last of August on a weekend on a Friday where...

Someone died...
A lot of blood...
Well, not a lot of blood considering...

Pause.

Where is Eddy?
Sometimes if you just keep talking, it will come to you...
It doesn't always work.

JEM stares at KATE. She has made her way to the foot of the steps leading to the level before the French doors.

It's hard to tell, you look alike, one like the other and then it's always dark. You play little games, on the game? Test questions, any question, to see if it is or it is not...

He tentatively reaches out as if to touch her.

Are you the one I arranged for?

KATE
Yes sir.

KATE steps up on the first step.

JEM
(*taking a step up*) Good. I spoke to you and told you what I
wanted, was that the way it went?

KATE
Yes sir.

*KATE steps up on the second step. JEM steps up on the
second step as well.*

JEM
Good. And what else? Was there anything else?

KATE steps onto the level in front of the French doors.

KATE
No sir.

JEM
Good.

He steps up to the level as well.

Nothing else no little ... no nothing, propositions made, declined,
accepted...

He glances back to the dust-sheeted table with the parcel.

Well you're here, aren't you? You are here arrangements were made
as you can see...

*He indicates the room, moves down, removes the crimson
dust sheet from the pouffe, and drapes it around himself
like a toga. KATE tries to open the French doors.*

Harry's left everything covered. You can see that. I assume you can
see it. I can see it. Although that is not always the best test...

He notices KATE trying to open the doors.

He has his people Harry, his man, and a woman who comes in,
they come in and prepare things for the weekend, he comes to

Chiswick on the weekend but not this weekend. He's left things up to me and I have arranged for you.

JEM indicates for KATE to sit and he sits on the pouffe he's uncovered. She sits in the chair. He is looking at the dust sheet, one hand holding it up for examination.

What colour are the dust sheets? ... That is not a test question.

KATE

(*glancing at the dust cloths*) ... White sir.

She laughs. He speaks to his hand under the dust sheet, working it as if it's a puppet.

JEM

I should not mind
If you were done away with, killed, or plowed.
You do not seem to serve a useful end.
And certainly you are not beautiful.

KATE

Is there another colour you'd prefer, sir?

JEM

The colour is unimportant. The intellect is unimpaired.

KATE

If you say so, sir.

JEM

There's the rub. You've put your finger on it and don't think I don't think about that. Would an impaired intellect recognize it's impairment? Might, perhaps, the failure to recognize be the most compelling symptom of its impairment, everything starts at home! On the other hand, the unimpaired intellect can state with certainty, "The intellect is unimpaired." In either case the intellect's assessment is "The intellect is unimpaired," so one can tell nothing from that. It seems the only proof of the soundness of one's intellect would be the firmly held belief that one's intellect is impaired!

Pause.

I don't subscribe to that belief.

Pause.

Which leaves the impairment of my intellect an open question, I think we can at least agree on that.

He leans forward and whispers.

The heir presumptive to the throne of England, Prince Albert Victor Christian ... Edward, will honour the premises with his presence this evening.

KATE
(*impressed, possibly excited*) Yes, sir.

JEM
You must help me.

KATE
Yes sir.

JEM
I've made arrangements for it, haven't I?

KATE
Yes sir.

JEM
It reduces me to rely on the likes of you. I abhor you, you are beneath contempt, had I the strength I'd tilt your head and slit your throat, but I consort with you to save Eddy, it must be done and I must do it. Are you close? ... Come closer.

She doesn't move.

You're not afraid?

KATE
No sir.

JEM
Good. Although it leads one to suspect your intellect. We will never speak of what transpires here this night, it will die with you.

A hint of uneasiness from KATE, he hastens to assure her.

It will die with all of us.

Knowledge is a terrible thing. It calls for action. And one must act or not act, and live with that.

Montague has been a friend, but you would know nothing of that, of friendship, love, nothing. You are a dosser, a daughter of joy, you sail along on your bottom and your life is savage and short and so it should be.

> *KATE stands.*

KATE
Thirty-five years old, sir. Given my circumstances, my health's considered good, sir.

JEM
Twenty-nine, and years older than you. My health is good, my intellect is unimpaired – I've got you there... come closer.

> *A moment, then she steps closer to him. He pushes her hat off and touches her head where he had formerly indicated the site of his head injury.*

A turning blade aged me.

> *He applies pressure and throws her to the floor.*

I have it over you there.

> *He throws the dust sheet he has wrapped around himself on top of her. A figure, EDDY, approaches the French doors, and unlocks them. KATE scrambles up to leave.*

My name is James Kenneth Stephen, Cambridge tutor to the heir presumptive to the throne of England!

EDDY
Hello Jem.

> *A warmth, a sense of intimacy, pervades the room with an accompanying change in JEM. The lights grow warmer. KATE's desire to leave is reduced by the presence of the prince. The prince is dressed for a more formal occasion.*

If I – If I said it was easy to slip away I'd be lying.

JEM
But you're good at that, aren't you?

EDDY
Good at what?

Holds his hat and gloves out which KATE takes.

JEM
Slipping away.

EDDY
(*laughs*) You know I am.

JEM
I knew you'd come.

JEM removes EDDY's cloak and tosses it to KATE. She places the cloak, hat, and gloves, on the chair by the French doors. She removes the dust sheet on the chair and table with the parcel, dropping the crimson sheets to the floor. During the following, she will take her carpet bag, remove the sheet from the chair extreme downstage left, and open her carpet bag. She will make some changes to her wardrobe, i.e., her shoes to boots; add a rough apron with a bonnet attached to it; a pair of gloves with no fingers; a red handkerchief around her neck.

EDDY
Of course it wasn't easy. Eventually they'll miss Prince Albert Victor, but no one'll notice Eddy's gone.

JEM
Oops! Gone!!

EDDY
Pardon?

JEM
Slipped away –

JEM leaps up on to the pouffe, making a gesture as if to catch something.

Oops gone!

He jumps off the pouffe.

EDDY
(*laughs*) Where's Harry?

JEM
Unable to join us, but here in spirit, oh yes.

EDDY extends his hands and JEM grasps them.

EDDY
You look well.

JEM
Do I? I do. We must talk, Eddy, and you must be honest with me.

He sits EDDY down in the chair by the small table.

EDDY
Of course. Where are the others?

JEM
The others.

EDDY
Our apostle friends. I thought Harry would be here, I thought everyone would –

JEM
No. Only us. We two at the moment. James Kenneth and Albert Victor. And we will speak frankly to one another, won't we.

EDDY
If you say so.

JEM
You are the future king of England and the Empire, the greatest empire the world has ever known.

As JEM speaks EDDY's attention wanders, eventually to the parcel on the table.

And I am your intimate friend who at some future date will play a role yet to be determined in the governance of this great Empire. Since Elizabeth the first ... the first –

EDDY picks up the parcel. JEM takes it from him and puts it on the pouffe.

that has been my family's role – to serve the monarchy, and it's my role on grounds that far exceed the rote and role of family.

EDDY
Don't put on your robes and play the teacher, Jem, we're not at Cambridge now.

JEM
We have to talk.

EDDY
But it bores me. You know it does.

JEM
Concentrate the mind, Eddy, think!

EDDY
I come here to escape all that, why aren't the others here?

JEM
One is coming. You are the heir presumptive to the throne of England –

EDDY
Who?

JEM
You will be King!

EDDY
I know that. Who else is coming?

JEM
Montague.

EDDY
I like him. He may not be Cambridge but Oxford is just as good.

JEM
It's important we talk!

EDDY
Talk then! But talk about something interesting!

JEM
Eddy.

EDDY
You say I will be King, then treat me like a King.

He gets out a cigarette.

JEM
To be! Presumptive!

JEM lights EDDY's cigarette.

EDDY
The King is not interested in discussing things political or intellectual this evening.

JEM
If things political or intellectual are not of interest, what is of interest to Your Highness?

EDDY
I don't know... Hunting!

JEM
Aah.

EDDY
Two hundred and forty-eight pairs of quail yesterday, what do you think?

JEM
A fair number.

EDDY
And if we hadn't run out of cartridges, it've been five hundred.

JEM
Indeed.

EDDY
You see. There's something I do well.

JEM
Kill quail.

EDDY
And other things, larger things, more dangerous.

EDDY's gaze returns to the parcel.

JEM
I suspect so.

JEM picks up the parcel and sits in the chair at extreme stage right.

EDDY
And people say Prince Albert Victor is a superb horseman. And they're right I am. I could give you lessons.

JEM
Oh yes.

EDDY
You could have used them. You can be the pupil and take instruction. I don't think you'd be good at it.

JEM
We have to talk, Your Highness.

EDDY
You know I don't like that here, call me Eddy.

JEM
Eddy, listen.

EDDY
No. Why is no one here? Where's Montague?

JEM
Eddy –

EDDY
If this is all there is, I'll slip away to London, I'll slip away to Cleveland Street and the rent boys there.

JEM
Or Whitechapel, Eddy?

EDDY
If I should care to.

JEM
I'm trying to save you, Eddy. And save myself. You're right about my horsemanship. The horse escaped scot-free, and here I am hanging on – an act of intense concentration – motivated only by my love of you, my great love of you. Look. Look.

He indicates his head.

EDDY
You've changed.

JEM
No.

EDDY
I liked you better before.

JEM
Only liked... and before what?

EDDY
Before. At Cambridge. You were nicer then. You introduced me to people who became my friends, I learnt how to play whist and a lot of other things that I enjoy now that I didn't know about before. I found myself. You were my tutor and I learnt I could do what I want.

JEM
But always governed by this, Eddy, (*he taps his temple*) by this.

EDDY laughs a small laugh and moves to the sideboard to pour a drink. JEM rips the paper off the parcel in his lap. He opens a case. The interior lining of the case is stained with blood. It holds two knives, the blades six to eight inches long. He points one knife at EDDY.

Eddy!

EDDY turns and JEM makes a vicious gesture with the knife in his other hand at KATE.

You!

KATE
I'll soon get me doss money, see what a jolly bonnet I've got now?

Two pence a poke and four pence a bed, I've earned money for a doss bed three times over today and spent it all on drink!

She laughs, then sings.

I pray you lord for Jesus' sake
Give me this day a little cake.

She focuses on **EDDY** *and moves towards him.*

Hallowed be Your Highness's name
But don't forget to send the same.

To **EDDY.**

Call me Polly. Can I help you? Is there anything I might have you might want?

EDDY *gives a brief look and a small smile to* **JEM.**

I was a good girl once but me old man ran off with me best friend who acted as midwife when Sarah was born – Oh he come back. They always come back. I wish to God he'd stay away.

She sings.

Oh hear me cry Almighty Host
I quite forgot the quail on toast
Let your kindly heart be stirred

She glances at **EDDY'**s *crotch.*

And stuff some oysters in that bird.

She makes a movement with her hips; **EDDY** *is not so much at ease.*

So he comes back and I have another one – the little boy who lives with me father now – and the old man kicks me out because a me drunken habits. He give me five shillings a week from his wages but he heard I was sailin' along on me bottom and he cut me off. I'd've done the same if I had the choice.

She touches **EDDY'**s *arm and he takes a step away from her.* **KATE** *registers that rejection. She sings again.*

Oh hear me Lord I'm prayin' still
If you won't help I guess I will

She focuses on JEM.

Put out in alleys and the street
Despite a fear of who I'll meet.

A toff, ohhh a toff, and a fine one too, a toff down in the Sinks to
see the sights!

She moves towards JEM who slips out of his jacket.

Were you huntin' for me, sir, or the likes of me?

She touches his knee, he pushes her hand away.

A tuppence sir, and I'm yours. That's the price and that's the way
and you won't regret it.

She bends over in front of him hiking her skirts up.

Up and out and in, with the cry a slaughtered horses ringin' in me
ears, and the press a Buck Row bricks markin' me back –

*JEM pushes her away with his foot against her derriere.
As she continues to speak, JEM looks at EDDY who watches.
JEM gets up, the knife in his hand, and approaches KATE
from behind.*

But hold – look – look at the sky, it's glowin', yes it's... there's a
wonderful fire down on the docks and it's lightin' up the heavens,
oh I wish I could be there, see the flames feedin' on wood, reachin'
up over the water, the water and fire and wood, wish I could be up
close, right in the middle, surrounded by flames burnin' in hell and
floatin' to heaven on a spire a golden smoke.

*KATE turns to find JEM behind her, he grabs her by the
throat, pulls her towards him, knees her in the stomach, she
grunts and drops to her knees. KATE and JEM's gaze lock
on each other. He illustrates the following with the knife.*

JEM
There is a slight laceration of the tongue.

KATE

Two or three inches from the left side of the abdomen...

JEM

A bruise running along the lower part of the jaw, a circular bruise on the left side of the face.

KATE

A deep wound, and several incisions running across the abdomen.

JEM

On the left side of the neck, one inch below the jaw, an incision four inches in length, on the same side an inch below it...

KATE

Three or four similar cuts running down the abdomen.

> *JEM hauls KATE to her feet and, swinging her round, reverses their positions.*

JEM

A circular incision terminating three inches below the left jaw.

> *He releases her, pushing her away, and thrusts the knife towards her in an upward gesture.*

Tissues are severed down to the vertebrae.

KATE

Tissues are cut through.

> *JEM turns to EDDY, the knife extends towards him.*

JEM

Is that how it was?

EDDY

That's how they say it was.

> *KATE sits on the chair at extreme stage right.*

JEM

What do you say?

EDDY

I say nothing. You're the one that knows.

JEM

Why do you say that?

EDDY

What would you have me say?

JEM

What do you know that I don't know?

EDDY

Nothing.

JEM

Nothing.

EDDY

Can the pupil surpass the teacher? I think not... except... in those areas in which the pupil excels.

JEM

Which are?

EDDY

Horsemanship for one.

JEM

You're a little shit!

EDDY

I'm bigger than you are.

JEM

Were you in Bucks Row on Friday night, August 31st?!

EDDY

No. Weren't you?

JEM

It's important I know. I can't help you unless I know.

EDDY

But you do know.

JEM

You remember re... member Harry?

EDDY

Of course I remember Harry.

JEM

Well Harry – Harry has shared certain information with me, information he's heard at the Home Office, information regarding suspicions – information regarding the identity of the Whitechapel murderer – at the moment Harry and other important personages are able to contain the investigation, contain it! But no, not for long, no cannot for long continue, indefinitely no! No!

EDDY

And this is of concern to you?

JEM

Of course it is!

EDDY

You seek my assistance.

JEM

Yes, Eddy, yes!

EDDY

Based on our former friendship.

JEM

No! No!

He sits on the steps before the French doors.

EDDY

What is it? ... What's wrong?

JEM shakes his head. EDDY sits down beside him and puts his arms around JEM's shoulders.

What's the matter?

KATE stands, watching them for a moment and then sings.

KATE

There's no time to tell you how
He came to be a killer
But you should know as time will tell
That he's society's pillar

For he is not a butcher
Nor yet a foreign skipper
He is your own lighthearted friend
Yours truly, Jack the Ripper.

> *She turns and sits on the pouffe. JEM looks at EDDY, then*
> *passes him the knife. EDDY stands up. He addresses KATE.*

EDDY
What do they call you?

KATE
Annie Chapman, guv'nor and some calls me Dark Annie and some
calls me Siffy.

> *She stands tentatively, moves to centre stage, facing out.*
> *EDDY is on the top of the level, behind her.*

I've flowers if you've a mind to buy 'em, crochet, antimacassars,
sell 'em – and matches too – but there's never enough and I'm sick
and I'm tired – but I can't give up, I got to go on ... I'm five foot tall
and some says I'm stout – but it don't come from food I can tell
you that. Me hair's dark brown and wavy and me eyes are blue and
once I was pretty ... I got a black eye and bruise on me chest from
a fight with Eliza Cooper, 'cause I seen her take a florin from Harry
the Hawker and give instead a polished ha'penny. They're keepin'
me bed at the doss house and if you're thinkin' a askin' me will I –
I will.

EDDY
But where Dark Annie?

KATE
Anywheres, guv, 'gainst a wall, down a passage, into the yard back
in this house, 29 Hanbury Street's good as any.

> *She speaks with a minimum of movement, physically stylized.*

Open the door that fronts on the street ... and close the door that's
what we does.

The door to the yard ... and close the door –
three stone steps down ... to the right of the stones
a small recess and a wooden fence

when I turns and looks in his face
a fist clutches me heart and squeezes
I look quick up at the sky –
showin' the soft flesh a me throat –
Everything
Stops.

JEM

(*to EDDY, as he sits. EDDY is still standing on the level*) Evidence
of suffocation, throat cut as before, the abdomen laid open, the
intestines severed from their mesenteric attachments and placed
on the shoulder of the corpse whilst from the pelvis, the uterus, its
appendages, the upper portion of the vagina, and posterior two
thirds of the bladder are missing.

KATE

(*again stylized*) Me rings are gone, two brass rings a value to no
one but me. Me hand is bruised, I put it up though I never knew
that I did.

> *EDDY puts his hand in his pocket, removes two rings,
> looks at them.*

A piece a muslin, a comb, and a paper case,
A coupla coins, two pills wrapped in an envelope that's torn,
What I was wearin'...
All of it makin' up me earthly goods.

> *EDDY moves, placing the knife and the two rings on the
> sideboard.*

JEM

Eddy?... Where did you get the rings?

> *KATE turns slightly on hearing this. She sits in the chair by
> the small table, listening but ignored by JEM and EDDY.*

EDDY

Where did you get the knives?

JEM

You must throw everything away.

EDDY

But that's not what you do is it?

JEM

The knives I found in a place which would be highly incriminating and indicating a particular individual. At some risk to myself – to myself! – I have wrapped and conveyed them here, brought them here!

EDDY

I slipped my hand in my pocket, there they were, two rings of some cheap metal.

JEM

Were you on Hanbury Street on Saturday, September 8?

EDDY says nothing.

Was I?

EDDY says nothing; JEM asks KATE.

Was I?

KATE says nothing.

I was not!
Do you love me, Eddy?

EDDY

I have a deep affection for you –

JEM

Nooo! Do you still love me! Love me! Don't talk about that deep affection shit! What's wrong with you, what've they done to you! I ask a simple question it has nothing to do with the death of five dregs from the East End slums – the world is better off without them, they foul the air when they draw breath! Do you think I care about them? There is waiting in the wings one hundred thousand others to take their place, the line is endless! I am talking about you and me and what I am willing to do for you to prove my love, to damn my soul, to kill for you, to save Eddy!... Do you love me!... It is a simple question.

Silence.

Once you would have answered before the words had left my lips.

Silence.

EDDY

(*a kind of explanation, or apology*) Mama is deaf. In one ear. That's a confidence and I charge you with respecting it. I am not deaf in either ear – but sometimes when things around one are not to one's liking, a partial deafness is not a disability...

JEM does not respond.

I was born two months before Mama's time, nothing was prepared for me, and the reverse has been true ever since. I'm prepared for nothing, but in time I get a sense of things. Not as you do Jem. Not an intellectual appreciation but an understanding. I understand the boar when it's been run to ground, can run no further, knows it must lie down, and what will surely follow.

I understand that sort of thing. And I recognize it.

You speak of saving me, killing for me, your love of me, the damnation of your soul on my behalf. Since Cambridge I have lived a little. I am Prince Albert Victor and certain things that once were cloudy clear a little. I do what I want, as Papa does.

JEM

Your father is an ass!

EDDY

My papa is the Prince of Wales and you will not speak of him in that way! You – you write poetry and publish books and practice law and teach and people call you brilliant. No one calls me brilliant, yet it is me who will be King. And when there's a bit of weather up, I do have sufficient sense not to back my horse into a windmill!

Pause.

If I were to think about it, I think I'd think that this is some elaborate ploy to bind me to you, not out of love, but out of desperation.

JEM

No.

EDDY

For your position has surely changed since first we met. Come now, sit and listen.

JEM does not move to sit beside EDDY.

I don't need saving. My position assures my safety. I can think of no military undertaking that we're engaged in or for which you would be suited, so who and how you plan to kill is something else that's quite beyond my power of comprehension. And pray do not damn your soul for me. I have a soul and it can seek its own damnation should desire dictate such an action.

JEM

And has it?

EDDY

(*smiles*) You mustn't try to catch me up. You may be smart, but I'm cunning.

JEM

I do love you.

EDDY

And I have a great affection for you. Take what's offered. And when I ascend the throne, there'll be a place for you. And Harry too.

JEM holds up the two rings.

JEM

There's danger, Eddy!

He places them on the small table beside KATE. She looks at them but doesn't touch them.

You must believe me. Listen! We must, before Montague, Montague arrives, we must – I've started wrong – it doesn't hurt – (*he touches his head*) – my intellect is unimpaired, I struggle but I prevail! It's our survival, yours and mine, not Red Jack, Spring Heel Jack, Saucy Jack, or Jack the Ripper's.

JEM notices KATE and speaks more intimately to EDDY.

Harry tells me he believes it's one of us. Someone's been seen.

EDDY
One of us?

JEM
They have a witness.

EDDY
(*smiles*) The intellect is impaired.

JEM
Perhaps! But Harry's isn't! Now do you understand?

EDDY
Harry says they have a witness.

JEM
And we must work together. To save each other.

KATE
(*speaking softly*) Double event this time.

EDDY
Witnesses to what?

       KATE slips the rings on her fingers and moves from her chair.

JEM
30 Berner Street.

EDDY
The International Workers Club.

JEM
You know it.

       He pulls out a document and refers to it.

30th of September
1888
12:45 a.m.
Sunday.
It is the evidence of Israel Schwartz
that at this hour
he did see
a man stop,
a man speak,

a man seize
and strike and throw –
the woman screamed three times
but
not
loudly.

KATE

(*sings*) We have fed you all for a thousand years
And you hail us still unfed
Though there's never a pound of all your wealth
But marks the workers dead.

> *The song strengthens in intensity and she moves towards EDDY.*

We have yielded our best to give you rest
And you lie on crimson wool

> *EDDY stands and takes a step away from KATE. She stops him with the next two lines of her song.*

But if blood be the price of all your wealth
Good God we have paid in full!

> *EDDY quickly moves away. JEM moves after him, touching KATE in approval on the shoulder as he passes her. He thrusts the document at EDDY.*

JEM

Observing Schwartz
the man called to a second man,
Schwartz walked away
but finding he was followed
by the second man
he
ran –
the woman
screamed three times
but
not
loudly.

KATE sings, much more aggressively, accusingly towards
both EDDY and JEM.

KATE
There is never a mine blown skyward now
But we're buried alive for you!
There's never a wreck drifts shoreward now
But we are its ghostly crew!
You have taken our lives and our babes and our wives
And we're told it's your legal share
But if blood be the price of your lawful wealth
Good God we have bought it fair!

JEM moves towards KATE threateningly. She drops her
accusing role, taking on the character of the next "victim."
She plays to both EDDY and JEM who is appeased, even
amused, by this offering.

You can hear it, hear them singin', outside the gate you can hear it.

She uses the French doors as if they were the "gate."

I'm out for a trade but I stop and listen, and sometimes I dance
'cause I got *looong* legs and curly black hair and a big fat lip that I
say comes from being kicked in the mouth clingin' to a funnel to
save myself when the Princess Alice sunk with the loss a 700 lives!

And it's all a lie. I tell terrible lies!

I say me husband drowned, and me children too! And everyone
knows I lie!

What's the harm? It's better than truth and what does that tell you
about what's real? I clean the doss house at Flower and Dean, I'm a
cheerful sort, me name's Long Liz and I don't look nothin' like that
picture they'll print a me. I got me lip from a fight way back when
and it healed like that, but don't you tell...

Look what I got!

She holds out her clenched fist to JEM who moves closer
to examine it, she quickly puts her hand behind her back.
She's on the top level and he joins her there.

Fella bought me sweets – he says will you? I says yes! He says, oh you! You'd say anything but your prayers!

Ahh it's rainin' out. It's an ugly night – but they're singin' in there!

Cradle a Liberty Club! Socialist Club – gonna free us all – and they sing! To keep their spirits up – to help them believe – and I dance out here in the rain!

She flings out her arms and sings. JEM is behind her on the level; KATE is on a lower step. EDDY watches.

We've fed you all for a thousand years
And you hail us still unfed
Though there's never –

JEM reaches out grabs the scarf from the back and twists it, lifting KATE up on her toes as she gasps three times, and tries to get her hands between her flesh and the tightening scarf. JEM gives three strong jerks. KATE's hands fall away to her sides, she appears suspended from the scarf which JEM holds from behind. Silence as his head falls forward.

JEM
(*yelling at EDDY*) Heeey!

EDDY stares at KATE and JEM. JEM slowly lifts KATE's head by grabbing her hair and pulling her head up to reveal her face to EDDY. He releases KATE who sinks to the ground. Silence as JEM looks down at her. EDDY slowly approaches her. He looks at JEM. EDDY starts to move away. Suddenly KATE grabs his arm. He pulls, trying to escape.

KATE
Say boss!
You seem rare frightened.

Guess I'd like to give you fits but I can't stop long enough to let you box of toys play copper games with me!

She releases EDDY who stumbles away.

See you soon!
Bye boss!

EDDY goes to sit in the chair extreme downstage right.

(*to JEM*) Double event this time?

JEM

Some things must be settled first!

Moving to EDDY.

First –

EDDY

First there are court circulars, where I am and when.

JEM

And where are you tonight?

He makes a gesture.

Oops gone.

EDDY

I... need to think.

JEM

Let me do the thinking.

EDDY

You think too much. Your head is full of scrambled thoughts and I must think of where my interests lie.

JEM

Let me help you, Eddy, like before! They brought you to me, here they said, make a man of him, do you remember? They said you were dull-witted, slow, a dreamer – mentally defective Dalton said!

EDDY

Stop.

JEM

What is it?

EDDY

I think you must believe I'm as they describe me to say such things and not believe it hurts me.

JEM

I would never hurt you, you know that.

EDDY

It hurts me! And yet you say you love me.

JEM

You know I do.

EDDY

I know so much. It's hard to reconcile with my stupidity.

JEM

But you're not stupid! We proved them wrong! You flowered and flourished at Cambridge, and that was me, I opened up that door. (*he touches his temple*) I offered a hand, (*he places a hand on EDDY's knee*) you grasped it and together we proved them wrong!

EDDY looks at JEM's hand, and slowly pushes it off his knee.

EDDY

The thing about being slow is that it gives one so much time to study the quick.

JEM

I would not have as my dearest friend one who was slow.

EDDY

And I, despite the slowness of my wit, have noticed certain things.

JEM

I would not have as my dearest friend one who was dull-witted!

EDDY

Then perhaps you misinterpret our relationship.

JEM

And you dare to speak of pain that I cause you!

He pulls open his shirt.

Look! See! Feast your eyes! My heart is torn in two! Look! Does it drip blood! You tear my guts out and then you speak of pain that I cause you!

*He sinks into the chair extreme downstage left. JEM and
EDDY are directly opposite each other stage right and
stage left. Silence.*

EDDY

I don't say I never cared for you ... I don't say I do not care for you.
If that's of comfort ... I think you underestimate me, Jem.

He gets up and moves towards JEM.

You see what I have noticed is that you have more to gain from me
than I can gain from you. And this is true of everyone I meet. The
recognition of this simple fact represents, I think, the instinct of
self-preservation in royalty.

JEM

(*whispering*) Danger, Eddy, danger.

EDDY

Perhaps there is, but surely more for you than me! I feel quite
invulnerable. I have no secrets.

JEM

You lie and you know I know it.

EDDY

If I loved you, which I do not! and which you must accept! Surely
you'd test that love's perimeters!

*EDDY moves to leave but KATE moves first, picking up
his cloak, rolling it up as she speaks.*

KATE

I'm in love! I'm in love and me love's got no perimeters!

*EDDY looks to JEM for assistance and guidance, disconcerted
by KATE's retaining his cloak, then moves back into the
room. KATE stalks him.*

It's bigger than London and stretches further than Kent! That's a
long stretch when you're hoofin' it to pick hops and the weather
turns bad and back the two a you come with nothin' in your
pocket but a coupla pence and a pawn ticket for a shirt! And me
love's name's John and we pawned his boots and I said you go to
the doss house 'cause he's not well and I'll stay on the street. He's a

fine-featured man and he's got bright eyes and his last name's Kelly.
And I love him, oh I do, and he loves me.

She confronts EDDY.

Yes, love!
Looove!

She includes JEM in her confrontation.

Love love love love love!!
And when he saw me lyin' in the Golden Lane Mortu'ry there –

She throws EDDY's cloak to the floor centre stage.

disemboweled like a pig, with me eyelids nicked –

*She moves after EDDY in a more threatening way than
previously.*

and me poor nose cut off and the skin a me cheeks flayed and a
lobe a me ear caught in the folds a me skirt, he wept, he cried out,
and he went round to the constables there and he was worse for
drink and –

She rushes at EDDY.

he knocked them down and he yelled out loud, "If I was you and
charged with walking the Whitechapel beat –"

*EDDY has sought safety behind JEM's chair, KATE faces
JEM in the chair and EDDY behind it.*

"If I was the copper in Mitre Square when he struck her down and
ripped her up! I'd've killed myself!! I'd've killed myself!!"

JEM stands up. KATE backs down in a way.

"I'd kill myself!!"

*She retreats upstage. Pause as JEM and EDDY watch her.
She draws herself up and continues.*

His name's John Kelly! He's a good man. We had seven years
together. And there was never a time that I went on the street but it
pained him and it hurt him!

JEM begins to advance on her but she stands her ground.

36

But we had a desperate need for money!
For a bit a tea! Or a – or a piece a bread!

Or a doss bed when the weather was bad and he wasn't well, and
a single doss is four pence you know and it takes you two to get
you that!! It doesn't seem right. He worked hard. Porter he was but
there's not always work, and sometimes so weak he couldn't finish
the end of a day. But I loved him.

JEM is getting closer to her.

It was somethin' special. And he loved me. I could see it in his eyes.
Bright they were. And I could hear his cry when he looked down,
down at me face and he knew it was me. Catherine Eddowes!
Sometimes Kate! Sometimes Jane! Sometimes Mary Ann!
Sometimes Kelly! Catherine Eddowes, born Wolverhampton 1842;
died Mitre Square, Sunday, September 30, 1888.

*She runs, grabs the knife left on the sideboard by EDDY,
and turns on JEM pointing the knife at him aggressively.
She sings.*

Praise God from whom all blessings flow!

*Silence as she holds JEM at bay with the knife. A moment,
then JEM steps quickly forward towards the knife point.
KATE pulls it back, raising the point of the knife, no longer
a danger. JEM slowly removes the knife from her hand.
Once he has the knife, he speaks softly.*

JEM
Praise God from whom all blessings flow.

*EDDY sinks into the chair extreme stage left with a sigh of
relief. JEM makes a move as if to step away from KATE.
Then suddenly he advances on her quickly with the knife
under her chin, forcing her back, up on her toes to reduce
the pressure of the knife on her neck.*

EDDY
Jem!! Jem!!

JEM
What?

EDDY

I ... I have to go.

JEM pushes KATE away.

JEM

Not yet.

EDDY

It's late.

JEM turns from KATE, then swiftly turns back on her indicating that she move farther into the room which she does.

JEM

But it's not too late. I implore you to stay a while. Re...member Montague is coming.

EDDY

He is not!

EDDY makes a move towards the door, JEM moves towards him with the knife.

JEM

Oh yes. To see you. To see me. To tell tales of his marvellous achievements at Valentyne's School for Boys.

EDDY

If you don't care for him, why did you invite him?

JEM indicates for EDDY to sit which he does.

JEM

Ah, but I do care for him – and he cares for us – and so I asked him. We're all in this together.

EDDY

I've not acknowledged that.

JEM sits playing with the knife which EDDY finds threatening.

JEM

Do you think that matters? What we know we know.

EDDY
Where's Harry's man?

JEM
Why? ... Did you want something? ... I'll get it ... Someone will get it ... Well?

EDDY
I can't ... slip away forever.

JEM
Some do, some don't.

EDDY
My absence will be noticed.

JEM
If not documented.

EDDY
I wish Harry were here.

JEM
Harry's left everything to me! I told you that! There's concern at the Home Office! Justice must be done! Or something passing for it, you know how it is. Don't be so annoying. Think, for Christ's sake, think!

EDDY
But – Montague is coming?

JEM
Yes Montague is coming! I hope to find him more amiable and open. I hope to find his loyalty to the crown, and to you personally in particular, to be without bounds, without limits, without – without –!

EDDY
Is he to be subjected to this same ... charade?

JEM
Christ!

JEM jumps up, leaves the knife on the small table, moves away in exasperation.

Here I am with half a head and anyone could see I'm ill, love me or not, and still I have a better sense of what is real and what is not than him!

JEM looks from KATE to EDDY, he notices that the knife is gone. EDDY is now standing. JEM speaks to KATE extending his hand.

I may yet bring this off and save him, but still I can assure you, the Monarchy's in trouble.

KATE shows both hands, no knife. JEM turns to EDDY. Pause.

EDDY
Have you considered the possibility... your mind's given way?

JEM
I've considered nothing else, it presses on me, exactly that consideration.

EDDY
Then why pursue so vigorously this course of action, whatever it might be?

JEM
I'd be mad not to, Eddy. Too much at risk.

EDDY
But... Montague is coming?

JEM
He is.

He sits EDDY back down.

EDDY
Things will unfold quite differently with Montague.

JEM
I do not love Montague, and the role I have assigned him differs considerably from the one I thought you'd play.

He holds out his hand. EDDY slips the knife out of his sleeve where he had concealed it.

EDDY

I shall hold Harry accountable for this.

JEM

You should fall on your bloody knees and kiss his feet. You should kiss my feet.

> *He sits on the chair extreme stage right, **EDDY** on the pouffe, **KATE** is standing extreme stage left.*

Kiss my feet.

> *JEM points the knife at **EDDY**.*

Kiss my feet!

> *EDDY ignores him, JEM points the knife at **KATE**.*

Sing!

> *KATE stares at him but does not sing. JEM leaps to his feet moving towards her.*

Sing!!

KATE

(*singing*) Dear Mr. Lusk
Herein please find
Half a kidney cut from one
Preserved it just for you.

> *JEM stamps his foot in time to increase the rhythm and volume of the song. KATE continues a bit louder, faster.*

The other half I fried and ate
with butter and a bun.
It was very nice and
I may send the bloody knife
If you can wait a while
signed your own lighthearted friend
yours –

JEM

Stop! Get your bag!

> *KATE doesn't move.*

Get it!

KATE does so.

Open it.

She does so.

Remove what I asked you to bring.

She takes out four large rocks and places them on the table.

Look, Eddy, what do you see?... Eddy, look.

EDDY glances at the rocks.

Well?

EDDY
I see some stones.

JEM
How many pockets do you have?

EDDY
I don't know.

JEM
I speak of major pockets.

EDDY
I don't know.

JEM
Of course you do. Four, Eddy. Two in the trousers, two in the jacket.

Four pockets, four stones. Four which is not a magic number, merely the right number.

We, the two us, together, are going to greet Montague with a great deal of sincerity and goodwill and bonhomie, and then we'll have some chat, and then we'll have some drinks, and after that, after, that...

KATE holds up a small bottle of laudanum, a liquid opium derivative, and places it on the small table.

Montague will first doze off, and after that he'll fall into a sleep, a final slumber from – too many drinks, or – something in his drink or something – some ... thing ... and after that, I will place two of these stones in two of his pockets, and you will place two of these stones in two of his pockets, and when we have accomplished that we will roll him into the Thames.

And we will do that for you, to save you, whether you want to be saved or not, whether you believe you need saving or not. And we will do it for me whether I am worthy of saving or not.

We will do it together to save the throne of England and the British Empire, whether it deserves saving or not.

And if you wish to sit on the same, you will keep your mouth shut and help me.

JEM kneels looking at EDDY.

Look in my eyes Eddy, and see what I tell you is true.

MONTAGUE knocks on the French doors.

Here he is now.

KATE turns. Facing the French doors, she sings with increasing vigour and volume, a kind of desperate signal.

KATE
Dear Mr. Lusk
Herein please find
Half a kidney cut from one
Preserved it just for you
The other half I fried and ate
With butter and a bun.
It was very nice and
I may send the bloody knife
If you can wait awhile.
Signed your own lighthearted friend
Yours truly, Jack the Ripper.

As KATE sings, JEM replaces the knife back in the case with the second knife. He moves towards KATE to shut her up. MONTAGUE knocks on the door as he looks *through the glass. **JEM** places the case with the knives, not totally closed, on the fireplace mantel, and moves again towards **KATE**. **MONTAGUE** knocks again. **JEM** moves to the door with a hard glance to **KATE** before he greets **MONTAGUE**. The door is opened as **KATE** sings the last two lines of the song: "Signed your own lighthearted friend / Yours truly, Jack the Ripper."*

JEM

My good fellow, come in! It's Montague, Eddy! Say hello!

*Lights fade to black as **EDDY** does not turn to greet **MONTAGUE**.*

Eddy?

The end of Act 1.

Act 2

JEM
Eddy?

MONTAGUE
No please –

JEM
Be nice, Eddy.

MONTAGUE
Your Highness.

He kneels at ***EDDY**'s feet.*

It is an honour and a pleasure, as always.

EDDY
No... ceremony here, my friend.

*****EDDY*** *moves to the sideboard, away from* **MONTAGUE**.*

MONTAGUE
Not ceremony, Your Highness. Love and loyalty freely offered.

JEM
That's what I like to hear.

MONTAGUE
Have I offended?

JEM
Prince Albert Victor's feeling a little off this evening.

MONTAGUE
I see ... I trust your health will soon improve, Your Highness.

EDDY
Call me Eddy.

JEM
For it's just a wee informal gathering. Only you, me, and Eddy.

MONTAGUE
And Harry.

JEM
I'm afraid Harry won't be joining us this evening.

MONTAGUE
Oh. I did hope –

JEM
Shall we converse? With sincerity and goodwill?

MONTAGUE
I never know how to take you Jem.

JEM
As you find me. Is there any other way?

> *He leaps up on the pouffe and strikes a pose, hand on chest, and launches into a recital.*

"Ode to An Unknown Lad"

Shall I present a peppermint
As schoolboys love to suck
To this poor lad I've come upon
And dearly love to –

Oh – dear – a pale wash sweeps your face, Montague. Is it the quality of my verse?

> *MONTAGUE smiles and shakes his head.*

No? Ah-huh, I know –

> *He glances down at his attire.*

You note my somewhat dishevelled appearance and it dismays

you. I will explain, all will be made clear. At the end. One can only hope, after struggling through this vale of tears, one can only hope that the necessity of the journey, the meaning of the journey, will be made clear at the end, whether one rides a golden cloud into eternity (*this last is directed at KATE, who sits extreme stage left*) or plummets like a stone. Like a stone, Eddy! I am quick, aren't I? The intellect is unimpaired! – Plummets like a stone into the vaults of hell!

>*He sits extreme stage right.*

MONTAGUE
As always, a torrent of words, eh Eddy?

JEM
Aren't you staying?

MONTAGUE
(*laughs*) I think I will.

>*He removes his coat.*

JEM
(*to KATE*) His coat.

>*KATE doesn't move. MONTAGUE holds his coat for her to take.*

His coat!

>*She doesn't move; JEM quickly takes his coat. EDDY at the sideboard has picked up a glass and decanter.*

You missed the hors d'oeuvres, Montague, I had half a kidney (*as he throws the coat at KATE*) and Eddy? Eddy passed, Eddy is very secretive about his likes and dislikes, but Eddy knows what he wants, and at this moment, the prince desires a drink, you see I know his wants and needs better than he knows himself.

>*EDDY puts the glass and decanter down.*

But note, the prince restrains himself, he does not take a drink, and what is one to make of that?

MONTAGUE
You don't know him as well as you think?

JEM

I sometimes feel myself propelled to that conclusion. Earlier I tore my heart out and flung it on the floor and he trod on it!

MONTAGUE is amused; JEM appears swept up in an excess of energy.

It's here someplace. Under a chair, the sideboard, or in one of the corners. Tomorrow it will be swept up and tossed out with the trash! Unless, of course, that cat (*referring to KATE*) finds it first.

(*to KATE*) Now what was it Mary Kelly said?

He catches himself and moves to EDDY.

No, no, this is a royal story, Eddy, you should know it. Mary Mary Mary Queen of Scots or, Mary Queen – whose head was chopped off – no, what do people say she said about her heart, Eddy?

EDDY

I don't know.

JEM

He doesn't know. Christ. And me his tutor.

EDDY

At Cambridge.

JEM

Well at least he's got that right. There's hope for England yet. But here, here we have a master in our midst, a schoolmaster whose reputation has preceded him, what's the story concerning the Royal Mary's heart, Montague?

MONTAGUE starts to speak.

If indeed she had one.

MONTAGUE starts to speak.

Which I sincerely doubt.

MONTAGUE starts to speak, hesitates.

MONTAGUE

That...

JEM
(*simultaneous with* **MONTAGUE**) Well?

Brief pause.

MONTAGUE
One should find engraved upon it, "Calais."

JEM
Traitorous Catholic bitch!

MONTAGUE and JEM laugh; EDDY smiles.

But on my heart, if one could find it here, you'll see the imprint of a foot. No, not so clear as that. A number of indentations made by a pair of slim black highly polished boots, oh he danced a fair fandango on it.

He puts his hands above his head, jumps somewhat dance-like in front of EDDY, on the last "dah" he does a dance kick towards EDDY.

Da da da da da dah! Dah!

He and EDDY stare at each other. After a moment JEM turns to MONTAGUE reassuring him.

An illustration.

Removing one's heart, or anyone's heart for that matter, is not an easy job. Ask Eddy. He knows.

Go on, ask him.

MONTAGUE looks to EDDY. Pause.

MONTAGUE
I – respect the prince's reticence.

JEM
Oh he's "the prince" now, is he?

MONTAGUE
There are some things one may choose not to share in public forum. Eh Eddy?

JEM

Public forum? Christ! Who could be closer than the three of us?

MONTAGUE

Laughs.

You have an advantage.

JEM

And destined to be closer still before the night is out.

MONTAGUE

But I've come late. You're into play and I don't even know the rules.

KATE

Mary Kelly in Miller's court on a Friday, sir.
The extraction of the heart through the diaphragm
suggests to some
A degree a medical skill.
It was taken away.
The heart, sir.

JEM

Stop.

MONTAGUE

What did she say?

JEM

Oh you must run to catch up, Montague.

KATE

Catch me – if you can. Boss.

JEM

And we don't need rules to play, there are no rules for us. Rules are for schoolboys to keep order in the class, eh Montague, is that how you keep order in the class?

He advances on KATE.

And for the lower classes to keep order in the streets!

He moves to EDDY, scooping up the laudanum bottle on his way past it.

And for *games* and we play *no games* here!

He holds the bottle up to EDDY, MONTAGUE doesn't see it.

Are we to have a drink Eddy? You stand there like a stuffed Hussar. For God's sake, pour, or move and let one act who's able.

EDDY
I don't care for drink.

JEM
You simply haven't had the right drink. Move and let me pour.

EDDY
Protocol demands that no one drinks before the prince.

JEM
Our need for drink is great, Your Highness. Montague's and mine. I pray you drink or move.

EDDY
Until the *royalty* that's present drinks, nobody drinks, or sits or eats or –

JEM
Move!

He attacks EDDY to move him from the sideboard over which he's stood guard since the beginning of the act. MONTAGUE moves to restrain JEM as the dialogue continues.

EDDY
Your actions are traitorous!

JEM
Yours are futile!

JEM pushes himself away from MONTAGUE's grip.

EDDY
I may have a drink later! I don't want one now – I need time to think, give me time.

JEM
We'll die of thirst.

MONTAGUE

Come now.

JEM

Come now.

MONTAGUE

The prince is right. Surely we can wait for a drink.

JEM

A proper prince feels in his blood when desire or need stirs in his subjects, and then the prince initiates, and others follow, thinking, "He leads." He doesn't lead, he simply has the faculty of recognition. He senses the wave before it crests. The proper prince is a vacuum, he neither wants a drink or needs a drink, his action in taking a drink serves as a signal freeing us to act on our own desires and needs. We've bred the Royal Family just for that purpose, and Eddy is a particularly apt example in at least one respect. He has the vacuum down pat. Now we're working on the recognition of simple facts.

MONTAGUE

You insult the Heir Presumptive.

JEM

All I want's a drink.

EDDY

So have one. You have permission.

JEM

After all that.

He moves to the sideboard tossing the laudanum bottle in the air and catching it.

EDDY

Montague and I... will abstain.

He moves from the sideboard.

JEM

Ah well.

He pours himself a drink, tosses it down, pause.

You know... I think dear Montague would need a drink...
I understand there's been a change in his employment.

MONTAGUE
A private matter.

JEM
Apparently not so private as you think or would prefer. I know.

MONTAGUE
How?

JEM
Anything that touches Eddy, I know. I'm told. Important people tell
me. It comes to me in a dream.

MONTAGUE
(*attempting to quiet JEM*) What you speak of has no relevance
here this evening.

JEM
I disagree. You've placed the prince in jeopardy.

MONTAGUE
How?

JEM
(*to EDDY*) There he stands, Eddy, your supposed friend, your
friend whose despicable behaviour with boys has resulted in his
dismissal from Valentyne's school at Blackheath!

MONTAGUE
You lie!

JEM
I lie? I think not. Have you been dismissed or not?

MONTAGUE
I have, but on charges that cannot be proven. I was summoned to
Valentyne's office only yesterday, Eddy, accused on the evidence
of some pupil whose name was not disclosed, then summarily
discharged with no opportunity to defend myself! It was a travesty
of justice!

JEM

An abhorrent crime!

MONTAGUE

The charge is groundless! And I intend to challenge Valentyne! I don't believe the boy exists.

JEM

You'd challenge Valentyne?

MONTAGUE

First, to reveal the name of my accuser. I know there's no pupil who could make this charge. And why Valentyne has acted as he has, that's a question too.

JEM

Do you get the picture, Eddy?

MONTAGUE

What picture, Jem?

JEM

Here's Montague, your dear friend Montague whom you care for and who cares for you, Montague who's charged with criminal behaviour involving an innocent.

MONTAGUE

But I've done nothing.

JEM

Montague who, in defending himself, will set off scrutiny of the most intense nature, scrutiny of his friends and intimates, his every relationship, and most particularly his relationship with Prince Albert Victor Christian Edward! Can the prince's relationship with his male friends withstand such scrutiny?

MONTAGUE

What goes on here? I'm present because of an invitation extended in the prince's name, an invitation to an evening of entertainment amongst my dearest friends, and this is what greets me?

JEM

I protect the prince.

MONTAGUE

I'd think that here, more than any other place or amongst any other people, I'd find support and sympathy! I would not have asked for this or pleaded for it. I would have kept this problem to myself – although I did think I might speak to Harry for I know he's close to Valentyne, and could, perhaps, explain his actions.

JEM looks to EDDY and smiles.

But no. I've been brought here by a ruse, a conspiracy by friends I've loved and trusted, for some end that is unclear to me. And you whom I had thought a friend (*referring to JEM*) take up the cudgel and attack with knowledge of an event I thought was shared only between myself and Mr. Valentyne, so – where does your information come from?

JEM

A sparrow. And with the number of sparrows that exist in London, I'd say it's almost public knowledge now, or soon will be.

MONTAGUE

If that's so, it strengthens my commitment to challenge Valentyne.

JEM

No matter what danger such action poses for the Heir Presumptive?

MONTAGUE

I must defend my reputation!

JEM

So much for love and loyalty. Mark that, Eddy.

MONTAGUE

Love and loyalty? Valentyne has made a criminal charge against me which has no foundation in fact!

JEM

And in defending yourself, you expose Eddy to the possibility of an equally damning charge!

MONTAGUE

Charge the prince?

JEM

Or at least suspicion of behaviour deemed criminal by the law of the land! See Eddy, he bends his knee and mouths the words, but it is me who truly loves you and defends you and protects you! I will save you!

MONTAGUE

From what?

JEM

Be it a true or trumped-up charge, we have here a test of love and loyalty, and Montague has failed that test!

MONTAGUE

The charge is false!

JEM

There he stands revealed as willing to sacrifice Prince Albert Victor's interests to his own.

MONTAGUE

Not true!

JEM

In his mind, the interests of the Crown are subservient to that of Montague Druitt's, and he will act on that!

MONTAGUE

How dare you!

JEM

I dare! I dare much! Shall we now have drinks all round now, Eddy?

MONTAGUE

Is this false charge some test that's been initiated?

JEM

A preposterous suggestion.

MONTAGUE

I can't believe so cruel an act would meet with your approval, Eddy... Eddy?!

EDDY

I... authorized... no such test.

MONTAGUE

Do you believe that my confronting Valentyne constitutes a danger to the crown, Eddy?

EDDY

I... a... danger? (*moving to JEM*) ... in what way Jem?

JEM gathers his strength and attacks again.

JEM

Think, for Christ's sake, think! – Our parties here at Chiswick? – which Montague attends?

He wraps an arm around EDDY's waist, standing behind him, and gives him a small but definite thrust with his hips.

And Cleveland Street? With Montague and others, the highest in the land, in attendance. Myself for one, and Harry, to say nothing of yourself! Can you see that featured on the front page of *The Star* or by the Central News Agency? Sooner than be the means by which that story's told, I'd throw myself into the Thames!

MONTAGUE

I fail to see how my defence can lead to such revelations.

JEM

If he would sacrifice you, why not you him?

He sighs into his chair.

EDDY

I thought it was Whitechapel that concerned us, not Cleveland Street, and Chiswick.

MONTAGUE

Whitechapel?

JEM

The point is... the point is...

JEM pulls EDDY to his knees beside the chair; he whispers.

He stands revealed ... He doesn't care for you. Cast him off and share ... a drink.

> *JEM stares into EDDY's eyes, then turns to look at KATE.*

Help me ...
Sing ...

> *Pause. EDDY reaches and turns JEM's face back. JEM smiles when his eyes rest on EDDY again. JEM clasps EDDY's face in his hands and sings to EDDY softly.*

Two little whores shivering with fright
Seek a cozy doorway in the middle of the night.
Jack's knife flashes, then there's but one
And the last one's the ripest
For Jack's idea of fun.

> *Silence. EDDY removes JEM's hands, places them in his lap, and moves away from JEM. Pause.*

MONTAGUE
Jem? ... Jem?

JEM
Montague? Ah yes. A friend. A friend, Eddy.

> *JEM reaches to MONTAGUE with his hand. MONTAGUE does not take it. EDDY moves to JEM. He stands behind his chair, drawing JEM's head back against him, stroking JEM's hair with one hand, the other hand is almost clasped over JEM's mouth. Silence.*

MONTAGUE
Whitechapel, Eddy?

EDDY
It preys on his mind. I'm ... uncertain why.

MONTAGUE
Where are the others?

EDDY
There are no others. Just we two – and you – are here tonight.

MONTAGUE
How long has he been like this?

Silence. **EDDY** *doesn't answer.*

My mother, you know... she suffers similarly... although for different reasons – and so this sad state is one with which I am familiar... I wish I weren't... How unfortunate, particularly when one thinks of what he was...

MONTAGUE *is slowly circling* **JEM** *and* **EDDY.**

What's this?...

He picks up a stone, speaks to **JEM.**

Four stones?

JEM *turns his head to look at* **MONTAGUE** *holding out the stone to him; he says nothing.* **MONTAGUE** *puts the stone back on the table and moves away.*

It's distressing, and I expect most painful for you...

He almost steps on Eddy's cloak and avoids it.

who's been so intimate a friend... You and he have been so close... a great loss... is there anything I can do?

MONTAGUE *has ended up at the fireplace.*

My problem with Valentyne is somehow... placed in perspective... I know there is no truth in it, and the truth will out.

Leaning on the mantel **MONTAGUE's** *elbow nudges the knife case, he picks it up, it is not closed all the way. As he looks in it and takes out one of the knives,* **EDDY** *quickly moves to him, grabbing the case and taking the knife from him then moving back towards the sideboard.* **KATE** *stands.*

What's this?

KATE
A post-mortem knife, sir, which is specifically designed for ripping upwards.

EDDY moves towards KATE threatening her with the knife. He's stopped by MONTAGUE.

MONTAGUE
Whitechapel, Eddy! Is it possible?

EDDY
Of course not!

MONTAGUE
It is, I see it in your face!

EDDY
No! You misread me, and the knife is proof of nothing!

MONTAGUE
But you spoke of Whitechapel, and he –

EDDY
No. It's just a knife!

KATE
The case is lined with blue silk, sir.

EDDY
A case cannot be made on the simple possession of a knife!

KATE
The silk is heavily blood stained.

EDDY
Jem?!

KATE removes the rings from her hand and gives them to MONTAGUE.

KATE
Annie Chapman, sir!

EDDY
One could as easily say –

EDDY realizes he still holds the knife and case and hastily puts them on the sideboard.

– that you, because … because your father was a surgeon, and
mutilation played a role, that you're the one!

MONTAGUE
No, Eddy.

EDDY
I remember your cousin had a surgery in the Minories, a few
minutes from Mitre Square, and a most convenient hide hole!

MONTAGUE
It won't do, Eddy … I believe you suspect Jem.

He looks from the rings to **EDDY.**

I think you know.

EDDY *snatches the rings from* **MONTAGUE.**

EDDY
You make an incredible accusation against my friend!

JEM
Thirteen Miller Court! The room is twelve foot square. There are
four pieces of furniture, two tables, one chair, and a bed. She feels
secure.

KATE
Name her.

JEM
She disrobes.

KATE
Name her!

JEM
She lies on the bed.

KATE
Name her!

JEM
She cries, oh murder! Nobody comes, she is flayed and gutted,
nobody comes.

KATE

Name her!

JEM

Nobody comes.

KATE

Mary Jane Kelley!
Age 24.
Somebody's baby!
Somebody's daughter!
Somebody's love!

JEM

Nobody comes.

Pause.

MONTAGUE

He accuses himself.

EDDY makes a drink for himself and MONTAGUE.
He picks up the small vial JEM had left on the sideboard
and pours it into MONTAGUE's drink. As he does so,
KATE speaks intimately to MONTAGUE.

EDDY

But what is proven? That he reads *The Star*? And you read too
much in his ramblings.

KATE

(*to MONTAGUE*) The case holds a pair, sir.

EDDY

You spoke of our intimate friendship, Jem's and mine? Do you
honestly believe he could commit such acts, or act in consort with
another to –

He catches himself.

– commit such acts, and I not know it?

MONTAGUE

(*to KATE*) What do you mean?

EDDY
I mean nothing. I seek to reassure you.

KATE
There are two knives, sir.

EDDY
At last, a drink, I feel a thirst, and I appreciate your patience.
A drink – from the hand – of the would-be King.

> *MONTAGUE looks from KATE to EDDY, considers,
> makes his decision and moves from KATE to join EDDY.*

KATE
No.

EDDY
A toast … a toast …

MONTAGUE
To what, Your Highness?

JEM
(*to KATE*) To love and friendship.

> *MONTAGUE and EDDY drink. Once MONTAGUE
> has drunk, KATE moves to her chair, extreme stage left,
> and sits. Her carpet bag is there. JEM's gaze follows her.
> JEM still sits in his chair, languid, quiet.*

How is your mother, Montague?

MONTAGUE
Much better, thank you.

EDDY
I trust … you do feel reassured. You have my word that all is as it
should be.

MONTAGUE
He spoke of scandal that might ensue from this incident at school.

> *He takes a drink.*

What do you think would follow if suspicion as to the identity of
the Whitechapel murderer fell on one so close to you, Eddy?

A look to EDDY who stands close to him. Pause.
MONTAGUE slowly circles the pouffe.

And... there is... certainly a suggestion that – a second individual may be involved.

A look to EDDY across the pouffe. MONTAGUE puts a hand out to, perhaps, steady himself on the pouffe. Then moves to EDDY.

Harry... is close to things... you must ask his advice, if the investigation should... you must be protected, Eddy. You can rely on my discretion, Your Highness.

EDDY gives MONTAGUE a gentle touch, a stroke of MONTAGUE's cheek.

EDDY
I fear that is an accurate assessment.

Silence.

KATE
Shall I go now, sir?

JEM looks at her but doesn't answer. MONTAGUE finishes his drink, touches his head and sits on the pouffe; EDDY sits beside the pouffe. JEM in his chair watches them silently.

MONTAGUE
A multitude of thoughts press in... I fear I'm not good company tonight... I... request permission to take my leave...

Pause.

JEM
Prince Albert Victor gives his permission.

MONTAGUE slowly rises, makes his way to the sideboard, places his glass carefully on it. EDDY sits on the pouffe. Neither watch MONTAGUE as he slowly makes his way towards the French doors. He stops for a moment before carefully attempting the steps to the level. He sits down carefully on the level for a moment. After a moment he gets

*up and exits, shuts the door. Pauses for a moment outside,
then sits on the top step of the veranda.*

He'll sit on the outside steps... He'll rise again... A spreading
weakness in the left leg will result in a slight stagger which will
carry him onto the green...

MONTAGUE gets up slowly and moves out of sight.

The leg will give way... he will fall on one knee... the palm of each
hand will press on the grass... his right cheek will eventually rest
on the lawn...

Pause.

We will place the knives in their blue silk case in his rooms.

We will keep the rings.

I will pen a note, "Since Friday, I've feared that I'll become like
mother, and it is best for everyone that I should die."

We will place the note in his rooms.

*Silence. KATE gets up, picks up MONTAGUE's overcoat
from beside the chair in which she was sitting. She holds
out the coat.*

KATE
The body of Montague Druitt will be found floating in the Thames
at Thorneycroft near Chiswick on... Monday, December 31, 1888.
Four stones are found in Druitt's pockets. It is thought he suffered
from acute depression as a result of his recent dismissal from his
place of employment, and matters of a private nature. The finding
is death by his own hand.

She places the coat on the chair.

Police presence in Whitechapel diminishes.

*She recovers the chair with the crimson dust sheet which
is on the floor by the chair.*

Ripper investigations cease.

Pause. She turns to look at **EDDY** *who is looking towards her, sitting upright, still, on the pouffe. There is increasing hardness to her delivery.*

Prince Albert Victor will die on Thursday, January 14, 1892, at Sandringham from influenza and pneumonia, the onset of which terminated a most successful weekend hunt. His brother George will ascend the throne.

JEM turns in his chair to look at her.

James Kenneth Stephen will die on Wednesday, February 3, 1892, at St. Andrews Hospital, Northampton, from acute depression, melancholia, the refusal of all food, and dementia.

JEM
(*a small sigh and smile*) Ah yes.

> *He slowly gets up and makes his way to the sideboard.*
> *KATE picks up the crimson dust sheet and recovers the chair and small table. She picks up her bag and coat and starts to leave.*
>
> *JEM has picked up the knife from the sideboard. He points it at her.*
>
> *She looks at him for a moment.*
>
> *She looks at* **EDDY** *who sits immobile on the pouffe.*
>
> *She looks back at JEM who continues to point the knife towards her.*
>
> *She smiles, and leaves the room with no sense of fear, steps up onto the level, opens the door, closes it, disappears from sight. JEM follows her progress with the point of the knife but makes no move towards her. He is impotent despite the weapon.*
>
> *JEM turns back into the room, the knife ineffective, as lights fade on* **EDDY** *and JEM.*
>
> *Blackout. The end.*

SHARON POLLOCK's plays have been produced in the United States, Great Britain, India, Japan, and extensively across Canada. She was twice awarded the Governor General's Literary Award for her plays *Blood Relations* and *Doc*, the Nellie Award for National Radio Drama, the Golden Sheaf Award for her work in television, as well as the prestigious Canada-Australia Literary Award. In addition to her writing career, Pollock worked as an actor, director, and cultural commentator. She died in 2021.